PASSION FRUIT

DOUBLEDAY

New York   London   Toronto   Sydney   Auckland

PASSION FRUIT

ALEX GOTFRYD

PUBLISHED BY DOUBLEDAY
a division of Bantam Doubleday Dell Publishing Group, Inc.
666 Fifth Avenue, New York, New York 10103

DOUBLEDAY *and the portrayal of an anchor with a dolphin*
are trademarks of Doubleday,
a division of Bantam Doubleday Dell Publishing Group, Inc.

Library of Congress Cataloging-in-Publication Data
Gotfryd, Alex.
Passion fruit / Alex Gotfryd.—1st ed.
p. cm.
Includes bibliographical references.

1. Fruit—Literary collections.   2. Love—literary collections.
3. Cookery (Fruit)   I. Title.
PN6071.F76G68   1992
641.6'4—dc20   *91–25169*
                                                      CIP

ISBN   0–385–42069–2

Picture Research by Sabra Moore
Text Research by Jane Littell
Book Design by Marysarah Quinn

Copyright © 1992 by Doubleday,
a division of Bantam Doubleday Dell Publishing Group, Inc.
Photographs © 1992 Estate of Alex Gotfryd

All Rights Reserved
Printed in Hong Kong
May 1992

1   3   5   7   9   10   8   6   4   2
First Edition

ACKNOWLEDGMENTS

Victor Rodriguez

John Duff

Marysarah Quinn

Peter Kruzan

Peter Jones

INTRODUCTION

To eat figs off the tree in the very early morning, when they have barely been touched by the sun, is one of the exquisite pleasures of the Mediterranean. — ELIZABETH DAVID

Can any one of us not appreciate Elizabeth David's sweet remembrances—luscious grapes dusty from the vine, a succulent pear bursting with rich juices, the first sweet-scented strawberry of spring, the bright tang of a lemon. Whether eaten from the finest bone china plate or with gluttonous abandon fresh from the tree, the fragrance, the flavor, and the vision of some favorite repast linger.

Each fruit, common or exotic, has had its story told by poets, its beauty captured by the photographer's lens or the artist's pen, its essence re-created by countless cooks. And here, in *Passion Fruit*, is found the quintessential celebration of fruit: Alex Gotfryd's alluring images arouse the senses as they evoke the sight and taste of the bounty of the earth. The selections of prose and poetry from such diverse talents as John Milton, Mark Twain, William Shakespeare, and Wallace Stevens are fitting complements to the wonderful images. And, of course, no book on fruit would be complete without a few well-chosen recipes. From Jean Anderson, Judith Olney, Lidia Bastianich, and others come a host of mouth-watering selections to perfect the temptation of all the senses.

When one has tasted watermelons, one knows what the angels eat. It was not a Southern watermelon that Eve took: we know it because she repented.
— MARK TWAIN

I love you, Sunny :)
Love, Barbara

PASSION FRUIT

Passion Bubbles

SERVES 5

6 passion fruits
1 bottle (750 ml) champagne

Place a strainer over a medium bowl. Slice the tops off the passion fruits and scoop all the flesh and seeds into the strainer. With the back of a spoon press all the liquid through the strainer. Discard the seeds and remaining pulp. Spoon the passion fruit liquid into 5 heart-shaped ice cube molds (or other small novelty shapes). Freeze until firm. Pour champagne into 5 glasses. Remove fruit cubes from tray and drop one heart into each glass.

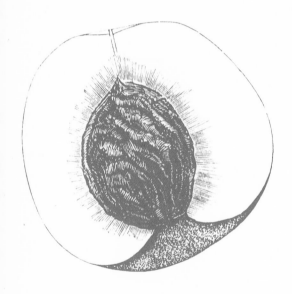

I asked a thief to steal me a peach:
He turned up his eyes.
I asked a lithe lady to lie her down:
Holy and meek, she cries.

As soon as I went
An angel came.
He winked at the thief
And smiled at the dame—

And without one word said
Had a peach from the tree,
And still as a maid
Enjoyed the lady.

—WILLIAM BLAKE,
  Poems from Blake's
  Notebook,
  "I Asked a
  Thief"

4

Almond Peach Cobbler

SERVES 4

4 medium peaches, peeled, pitted, and sliced

1 cup sugar

1 tablespoon flour

1/2 teaspoon cinnamon

1/4 teaspoon nutmeg

FOR THE TOPPING:

1 1/2 cups flour

1/4 cup sugar

2 teaspoons baking powder

1/2 teaspoon salt

1/4 cup butter, cut into small pieces and chilled

1/2 cup milk

1 teaspoon almond extract

1/4 cup chopped toasted almonds

Preheat oven to 400° F. In an ovenproof casserole combine peaches, sugar, flour, cinnamon, and nutmeg. Stir to mix. In a medium-sized bowl make the topping. Combine flour, sugar, baking powder, and salt. Add butter, and with a pastry cutter cut butter into flour mixture until it resembles coarse meal. Add milk and almond extract and stir just to mix. Spoon onto peaches. Sprinkle almonds on top, and bake 30 minutes, or until lightly browned.

Papaya "Salsa"

SERVES 4

2 papayas, peeled and diced
2 bananas, peeled and diced
¼ cup coconut milk
1 tablespoon minced fresh mint
2 cups cooked jasmine rice, at room temperature

Combine papayas, bananas, coconut milk, and mint in a nonreactive bowl. Cover with plastic wrap and chill at least 1 hour in the refrigerator. Serve over rice.

Kumquat Marmalade

MAKES 4 HALF PINTS

Make only small amounts of marmalade at a time so it doesn't scorch.

1³/₄ pounds ripe kumquats
½ cup lemon juice

1½ cups water
4 cups sugar

Halve the kumquats lengthwise, scrape out seeds, and core. Sliver fruit and rind together. Mix rind, fruit, and lemon juice in a very large, heavy enamel or stainless steel kettle, add water, and simmer, uncovered, 10 minutes. Cover and let stand in a cool place overnight. Next day, wash and sterilize 4 (8-ounce) jelly jars and closures, stand upside down on a baking sheet in a 250° F. oven until needed. Measure fruit mixture and for each cup add 1 cup sugar. Return to pan, insert candy thermometer, slowly heat, uncovered, to boiling, stirring until sugar dissolves; boil slowly, uncovered, stirring now and then, 30–40 minutes until thermometer reaches 218–220° F.; begin testing for sheeting.★ When marmalade is done, remove from heat, stir 1 minute, skim off froth, and ladle into jars, filling to within ⅛ inch of tops. Wipe rims and seal. Cool, check seals, label, and store in a cool, dark, dry place.

★ Take a small amount of the hot mixture on a cold metal spoon, cool slightly, then tilt. When drops cling together, forming a jelly-like sheet, jelly is done.

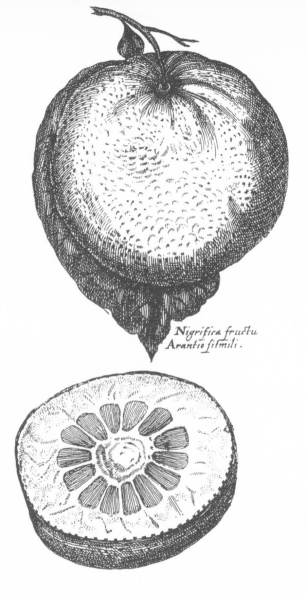

Nigrifica fructu
Arantio fimili.

Un orange sur la table,
Ta robe sur le tapis
et toi dans mon lit.
Doux présent du présent,
Fraîcheur de la nuit,
Chaleur de la vie.

—JACQUES PRÉVERT

That sunny dome! those caves of ice!
And all who heard should see them there,—
And all should cry, Beware! Beware!—
His flashing eyes, his floating hair!
Weave a circle round him thrice,
And close your eyes with holy dread,
For he on honey-dew hath fed,
And drunk the milk of Paradise.

—SAMUEL TAYLOR COLERIDGE,
Kubla Khan

Lemon Sponge Pie

SERVES 6–8

1 cup sugar
3 tablespoons all-purpose flour
Juice of 1 lemon
Finely grated rind of 1 lemon
1 large egg, separated

2 tablespoons melted butter
1 cup milk
Pinch of salt
1 unbaked 9-inch pie shell

Combine sugar and flour in a medium-sized mixing bowl. Stir in lemon juice and rind; beat in egg yolk, then melted butter. Stir in milk. Beat egg white with salt until fairly stiff peaks form, then fold into lemon mixture until no streaks of white show. Pour mixture into unbaked pie shell. Bake in moderate oven (350° F.) 35 to 40 minutes or until crust is lightly browned and filling puffy and touched with brown. Cool about 15 minutes before cutting. Good warm or cold.

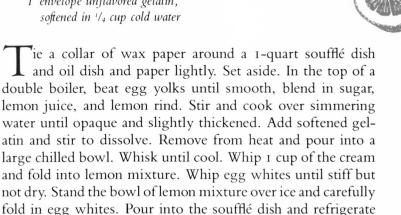

Cold Lemon Soufflé

SERVES 6

4 eggs, separated
1 cup sugar
1/2 cup fresh lemon juice
   Grated rind of 2 1/2 lemons, or
   1 1/2 tablespoons
1 envelope unflavored gelatin,
   softened in 1/4 cup cold water

1 1/4 cups heavy cream
2 ounces finely chopped or
   ground toasted almonds

Tie a collar of wax paper around a 1-quart soufflé dish and oil dish and paper lightly. Set aside. In the top of a double boiler, beat egg yolks until smooth, blend in sugar, lemon juice, and lemon rind. Stir and cook over simmering water until opaque and slightly thickened. Add softened gelatin and stir to dissolve. Remove from heat and pour into a large chilled bowl. Whisk until cool. Whip 1 cup of the cream and fold into lemon mixture. Whip egg whites until stiff but not dry. Stand the bowl of lemon mixture over ice and carefully fold in egg whites. Pour into the soufflé dish and refrigerate until set. Remove paper collar. Whip remaining cream and decorate top of soufflé with rosettes. Pat almonds around sides of soufflé.

with hugs & love —
Carole

Strawberries Romanoff

SERVES 4–6

1 quart fresh strawberries,
  washed, stemmed, and, if
  large, halved lengthwise
2–3 tablespoons superfine sugar
  (optional)
¹/₃ cup orange juice

¹/₄ cup curaçao
³/₄ cup heavy cream
2 tablespoons confectioners'
  sugar
¹/₄ teaspoon vanilla

Taste berries and, if tart, sprinkle with sugar. Let stand 10 minutes at room temperature, then toss lightly to mix. Add orange juice and curaçao and toss again; cover and chill several hours, turning berries occasionally. Spoon into a shallow serving dish. Whip cream with sugar and vanilla until soft peaks form, spoon into a pastry bag fitted with a large, fluted tube, and pipe cream over berries, covering completely.

Lichees in Port Wine

SERVES 4–6

*2 pounds fresh lichees, peeled,
    seeded, and halved, or 3 cups
    halved, drained, canned lichees
    (both are available in Chinese
    groceries)*
¹/₂ cup ruby port wine

Place lichees and port in a small bowl and toss well to mix; cover and chill several hours. Serve in stemmed goblets.

17

Crostata di Prugne

(PLUM TART)

SERVES 8

¹/₄ cup smooth apricot jam
One 10-inch tart shell, prebaked
    15 minutes
14 firm, ripe purple plums,
    halved and pitted

2 tablespoons sugar
¹/₂ teaspoon water
¹/₄ teaspoon lemon juice

Preheat the oven to 350° F. Brush 3 tablespoons of the apricot jam over the bottom of the prebaked tart shell. Starting from the outside edge of the shell, arrange the plums in concentric circles until the shell is filled. Bake the tart 10 minutes, sprinkle the sugar over the plums, and return to the oven for an additional 25–35 minutes or longer, depending on the texture of the plums, until the pastry is nicely browned and the plums are well cooked. Remove from the oven and cool.

In a small saucepan, melt the remaining apricot jam in the water and lemon juice. (Strain if the jam is lumpy.) When the tart has cooled somewhat, brush the plums with apricot glaze. Serve at room temperature.

Sweet Lou's Ripe Banana Cake

SERVES 10–12

2 sticks unsalted butter, at room
   temperature
1 1/2 cups sugar
2 eggs
1 teaspoon vanilla extract
1 teaspoon banana extract
3 ripe bananas with brown
   spots, mashed

2 1/4 cups cake flour
1/2 teaspoon baking powder
3/4 teaspoon baking soda
1/4 teaspoon salt
3/4 cup milk

Preheat the oven to 350° F. Oil or butter a 10-inch bundt or tube pan. Cream the butter and sugar together. Add the eggs one at a time, beating well after each addition. Add the extracts and mashed bananas. Put the flour, baking powder, baking soda, and salt in a bowl and give a quick stir. Alternately add the flour mixture and milk in 3 portions to the banana mixture, beating well after each addition. Pour into the prepared pan and bake for 50 minutes or until a testing toothpick comes out clean. Cool slightly before turning the cake out of the pan onto a cooling rack. This is a dense, rich cake. When cool, you can sift confectioners' sugar over the top as a finishing touch, frost the cake with your favorite buttercream icing.

And pluck till time and times are done
The silver apples of the moon,
The golden apples of the sun.
　　　　　—WILLIAM BUTLER YEATS,
　　　　　　The Wind Among the Reeds,
　　　　　　"The Song of
　　　　　　Wandering Aengus"

Love, to Sunny on her Birthday!
You are such a gift to us!
Cathy Parkins

A mother's hardest to forgive.
Life is the fruit she longs to hand you,
Ripe on a plate. And while you live,
Relentlessly she understands you.
　　　　　—PHYLLIS MCGINLEY,
　　　　　　The Adversary

20

Minted Apple-Lime Cooler

Bruise 2 mint leaves with ½ teaspoon sugar in a 12-ounce glass. Add apple juice or cider to half fill and mix well. Add 1 table-spoon lime juice and 2 or 3 ice cubes and mix again. Fill with ginger ale and add a wedge of lime.

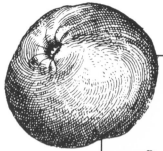

Baked Rome Beauty Apples

SERVES 4

4 *Rome Beauty apples*
4 *teaspoons raisins*
3 *cups water*
1 *cup brown sugar*

4 *perfect bay leaves*
4 *cloves*
1 *large pinch ground cinnamon*
2 *slices lemon*

Preheat oven to 350° F. Wash apples, cut out cores, and stuff cavities with the raisins. Place in a shallow baking dish. Combine remaining ingredients and pour over apples. Bake 30–40 minutes, until tender. Serve apples warm or cold, using a bay leaf on each for garnish.

In an orchard there should be enough to eat, enough to lay upon, enough to be stolen, and enough to rot on the ground."

—SAMUEL MADDEN,
quoted by Samuel Johnson.
From Boswell, *Life of Johnson*,
Vol. II

24

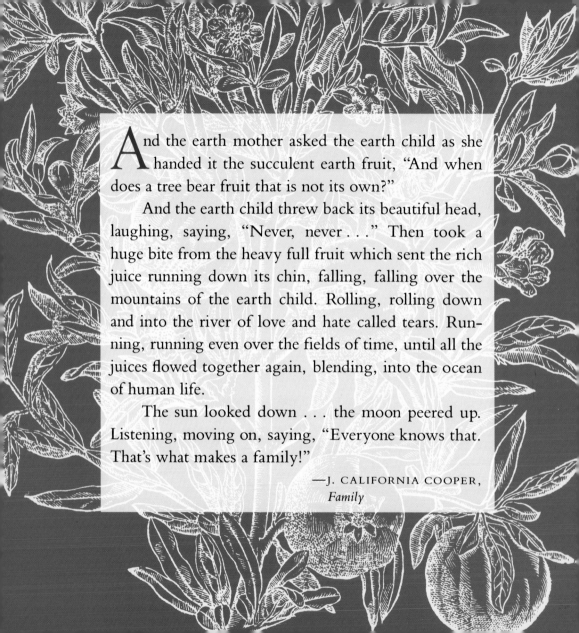

And the earth mother asked the earth child as she handed it the succulent earth fruit, "And when does a tree bear fruit that is not its own?"

And the earth child threw back its beautiful head, laughing, saying, "Never, never . . ." Then took a huge bite from the heavy full fruit which sent the rich juice running down its chin, falling, falling over the mountains of the earth child. Rolling, rolling down and into the river of love and hate called tears. Running, running even over the fields of time, until all the juices flowed together again, blending, into the ocean of human life.

The sun looked down . . . the moon peered up. Listening, moving on, saying, "Everyone knows that. That's what makes a family!"

—J. CALIFORNIA COOPER,
Family

Mrs. Hatfield's Ozark Pudding

SERVES 6

1 egg, well beaten
¾ cup firmly packed light
    brown sugar
¾ cup unsifted *all-purpose*
    flour
1½ teaspoons baking powder

½ teaspoon ground cinnamon
1 teaspoon vanilla
¾ cup finely chopped peeled
    apples
½ cup finely chopped pecans or
    black walnuts
Whipped cream

Beat egg and sugar well in a small mixing bowl; sift flour with baking powder and cinnamon and mix in. Stir in vanilla, apples and nuts. Spoon batter into a well-greased and floured 8 × 8 × 2-inch baking pan and bake in a moderate oven (350° F.) for 30 minutes or until crusty brown on top. Let pudding cool about ½ hour before serving. To serve, cut in large squares and top each with a drift of whipped cream.

Hidrapia
Ulmer Wasserbirn.

Pira Angelica magna.

Peras de Naranja

¹/₂ cup fresh orange juice	4 whole cloves
2 cups dry white wine	¹/₂ cup sugar
¹/₄ cup orange-flavored liqueur or Triple Sec	1 whole cinnamon stick
Rind of one orange	6 Bosc pears, peeled and cored
¹/₄ cup white raisins	

Preheat oven to 325° F. In a heavy, deep ovenproof saucepan or casserole combine the orange juice, white wine, liqueur, orange rind, raisins, cloves, and sugar. Simmer over medium heat until the sugar dissolves. Remove from the stove and add the cinnamon stick and the pears. Bake, covered, 40 minutes until the pears are tender. Cool the pears and liquid to room temperature. Refrigerate for at least 3 hours before serving.

Pira berilia
Herrnbirn

Pira biemalia
Winterbirn

No thing great is created suddenly, any more than a bunch of grapes or a fig. If you tell me that you desire a fig, I answer you that there must be time. Let it first blossom, then bear fruit, then ripen."

—EPICTETUS,
Discourses

Happy Birthday! Sweet Dear! with our love Bally

Oh those melons! If he's able
We're to have a feast! so nice!
One goes to the Abbot's table,
All of us get each a slice.
How go on your flowers? None double?
Not one fruit-sort can you spy?
Strange! — And I, too, at such trouble,
Keep them close-nipped on the sly!

—ROBERT BROWNING,
*Soliloquy of the Spanish
Cloister*

Celebration Day! August 19, 1993

31

Here are fruits, flowers, leaves, and branches,
And here is my heart which beats only for you.

—PAUL VERLAINE,
Romances sans paroles

With love,
Anne Nicolai

Papaya Sherbet

2 papayas
$1/2$ cup orange juice
1 tablespoon orange liqueur

$1/2$ cup sugar
$1/2$ teaspoon fresh lemon juice

Remove the seeds and skins from the papayas and dice them. Combine all ingredients in a food processor or mixing bowl and mix well until very smooth. Pour into a refrigerator tray or shallow pan and freeze until sherbet has the consistency of mush. Remove from freezer and stir vigorously. Refreeze until mushy again, repeat stirring. Return to freezer until ready to serve.

Blood Orange and Strawberry Compote

SERVES 6

6 blood oranges, washed
2 cups hulled ripe strawberries,
  sliced lengthwise

Sugar to taste
Kirsch to taste

Remove all the skin and pith from 4 of the oranges, and remove sections by cupping orange in one hand and slicing between membranes. (Work over a bowl to catch juice, and let sections fall into bowl. Remove seeds.) Squeeze juice from the remaining 2 oranges and add to bowl. Add strawberries. Toss gently with sugar—the amount depends on the sweetness of the fruit—and kirsch to taste. Chill for 1 hour.

Hot Fruit Compote

SERVES 6–8

1 pound small ripe peaches or apricots, peeled, pitted, and halved

1 pound small ripe pears, peeled, cored, and halved

1 pound small ripe plums, peeled, pitted, and halved

1 cup firmly packed light brown sugar

½ cup orange juice mixed with ½ cup water

¼ cup lemon juice

1 tablespoon finely slivered orange rind

2 tablespoons butter or margarine

Preheat oven to 350° F. Arrange fruits in a large casserole. Combine sugar, orange juice mixture, lemon juice, and orange rind; pour over fruits, then dot with butter. Bake, uncovered, ½ hour; serve hot with cream or cool and ladle over ice cream or pound cake.

ALL HUMAN HISTORY ATTESTS THAT

SINNER!– SINCE EVE ATE APPLES, MUCH DEPENDS ON DINNER.

—LORD BYRON, *Don Juan*

Happy happy B-Day
and may many
more!! Gill

38

I sing the fig, said she,
Whose beautiful loves are hidden.
Its flowering is folded away.
Closed room where marriages are made:
No perfume tells the tale outside.

— ANDRÉ GIDE

Eva Kirkland's Old-Fashioned Fig Preserves

MAKES 5 PINTS

3 cups water
6 cups sugar
4 pounds figs, rinsed and left whole

5 slices lemon, approximately ⅓ inch thick, seeded
5 pint-size mason jars with lids, sterilized

Combine the water and sugar in a large nonreactive pot. Bring to a good agitated rolling boil. Add the figs, cover the pan, and cook slowly for 45 minutes. Be sure to regulate the heat so that the fruit is at a bare simmer. After 45 minutes, remove the lid and add the lemon slices. Continue to simmer uncovered for another 45 minutes. Remove from the heat, cover the pot, and let stand overnight so the figs can soak up the syrup. The next day, bring the figs back to a brief simmer, then ladle them into sterile jars. Slip a slice of lemon down the side of each jar so it shows decoratively. Seal the jars. Mrs. Kirkland stores hers in the freezer.

The oranges of the Island are like blazing fire
Amongst the emerald boughs
And the lemons are like the paleness of a lover
Who has spent the night crying. . . .
                    —ABD UR-RAHMAN IBN
                        MOHAMMED IBN OMAR

40

Ambrosia

SERVES 6

4 large navel oranges, peeled
1/3 cup sifted confectioners' sugar
1 cup finely grated fresh coconut
    or 1 (3½-ounce) can flaked
    coconut

¼ cup orange juice

Remove all outer white membrane from oranges and slice thin crosswise. Layer oranges in a serving bowl, sprinkling with sugar, coconut, and orange juice as you go. Cover and chill 2–3 hours. Mix lightly and serve.

Shall I part my hair behind? Do I dare to eat a peach?
I shall wear white flannel trousers, and walk upon the beach.
I have heard the mermaids singing, each to each.

—THOMAS STEARNS ELIOT,
The Love Song of
J. Alfred Prufrock

Bibi Atallah
may there be
many more
and happy b.d.

Pesche con Mascarpone

(PEACHES WITH MASCARPONE)

SERVES 4

1 *cup fresh mascarpone cheese*
2 *tablespoons heavy cream*
4 *ripe peaches, halved and pitted*
2 *tablespoons chopped walnuts*
8 *strawberries*
4 *mint sprigs*

In a bowl, blend the cheese and cream. With a pastry bag, pipe the cheese mixture into the peach cavities (or use a spoon if you prefer). Sprinkle the walnuts over the cheese filling and serve two peach halves per portion, flanked by a pair of strawberries and a sprig of mint.

Mrs. McKamey's Open-Face Dutch Pear Pie

SERVES 6–8

1 9-inch unbaked pie shell with a high fluted edge

6 cups sliced, peeled pears (Bartletts make a particularly good pie; for 6 cups of sliced pears, you will need 6 large Bartletts)

1 cup sugar

6 tablespoons flour

1/4 teaspoon freshly grated nutmeg

Pinch of salt

1 cup heavy cream

Place a layer of sliced pears in pie shell; combine sugar, flour, nutmeg, and salt and sprinkle liberally over pears. Continue adding layers of pears and sprinkling with sugar mixture until pie is filled. Drizzle in the heavy cream. Bake pie in a moderate oven (350° F.) for about 1 hour or until crust is lightly browned and filling is set. Remove pie from oven and let cool at least 30 minutes before serving.

Nectarines Flambé

SERVES 4

1/2 cup butter (*no substitute*)
3/4 cup firmly packed light brown
    sugar
2 tablespoons lemon juice
4 large, firm nectarines, peeled
1/3 cup brandy or light rum

Melt the butter in a chafing dish or flameproof casserole (burner-to-table type) over moderate low heat, mix in sugar and lemon juice and heat, stirring until sugar dissolves. Add nectarines and simmer, uncovered, about 10 minutes, turning gently with a slotted spatula now and then, to glaze evenly. Warm brandy in a small saucepan, pour over nectarines, blaze, and spoon over nectarines until flames die. Serve at once.

47

Frozen Cherries Jubilee "Brûlée"

SERVES 4–6

1¹/₂–2 pints rich vanilla ice
    cream (depending on the
    size of your gratin dish),
    softened

¹/₄ cup kirsch, or to taste
2–3 cups halved and pitted Bing
    cherries
¹/₃ packed cup light brown
    sugar

Place the softened ice cream and kirsch in a bowl and work it with a heavy spoon until smooth. Stir in the cherries. Spread the mixture into a gratin or quiche dish and press the ice cream as flat as possible. Return the dish to the freezer for at least 1 hour (overnight is better). At dessert time, preheat the broiler until very hot. Press the brown sugar through a sieve in a light fluffy covering over the ice cream. Place immediately under the broiler just long enough for the sugar to caramelize into a brown crust, less than a minute—keep a close watch. To serve, crack the crust and spoon portions of crisp sugar and cold cherries in cream into serving dishes.

There is a garden in her face
Where roses and white lilies blow;
A heavenly paradise that place,
Wherein all pleasant fruits do grow;
There cherries grow that none may buy,
Till Cherry-Ripe themselves do cry.

—THOMAS CAMPION,
Fourth Book of Airs

Write me down
As one who loved poetry,
And persimmons.

—SHIKKI

Steamed Persimmon Pudding

SERVES 12

2 eggs
1¼ cups sugar
1¼ cups sieved persimmon pulp
(about 3 large ripe)
¼ cup melted butter
1½ cups sifted all-purpose flour
1½ teaspoons baking powder

½ teaspoon salt
½ teaspoon cinnamon
¾ cup milk
1 cup seedless raisins
½ cup chopped pecans (optional)
¼ cup brandy

SAUCE

1 cup sweet (unsalted) butter
2 cups sifted powdered sugar

2 eggs, separated
1 jigger rum or brandy

Beat eggs until light, then beat in sugar until smooth and lemon-colored. Combine persimmon pulp and melted butter and stir into egg mixture. Sift dry ingredients and stir in alternately with milk, beating well after each addition. Add raisins, pecans, and brandy. Transfer to a well-buttered mold and cover tightly with foil. To steam, set the mold on a rack in a large deep kettle and add water to come halfway up the sides of the mold. Bring water to gentle boil, cover saucepan, lower heat, and steam for 2½ hours. Remove pudding from water and let cool for 15 minutes. Unmold onto foil and cool completely if wrapping and freezing. Bring to room temperature before reheating. Serve warm with sauce. For the sauce: Cream butter and sugar until soft and fluffy. Beat in egg yolks one at a time, add rum or brandy, and mix well. Beat egg whites until stiff but not dry, and fold into sugar mixture. Serve at room temperature.

The month of May was come, when every lusty heart beginneth to blossom, and to bring forth fruit; for like as herbs and trees bring forth fruit and flourish in May, in likewise every lusty heart that is in any manner a lover, springeth and flourisheth in lusty deeds. For it giveth unto all lovers courage, that lusty month of May.

—SIR THOMAS MALORY,
Le Morte d'Arthur

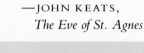

And still she slept an azure-lidded sleep,
In blanchèd linen, smooth, and lavendered,
While he from forth the closet brought a heap
Of candied apple, quince, and plum, and gourd;
With jellies soother than the creamy curd,
And lucent syrups, tinct with cinnamon;
Manna and dates, in argosy transferred
From Fez; and spicèd dainties, every one,
From silken Samarcand to cedared Lebanon.

—JOHN KEATS,
The Eve of St. Agnes

Grapes in Grappa

SERVES 2

12 grapes   Approximately 1¹/₂ cups grappa
2 tablespoons superfine sugar

Place grapes in a clean, wide-mouthed pint jar. Sprinkle sugar over, then add enough grappa to cover the grapes. Cover loosely with clean lid and let macerate on the counter for 1 week. Then cover tightly and place in dark pantry or refrigerator for 3 months. Serve in brandy snifters as a delectable digestif.

Six Old Granny Smith Apples
Baked in a Pie

SERVES 6

FOR THE PIECRUST:

1 generous cup all-purpose flour
1 teaspoon sugar
Pinch of salt

1 stick unsalted butter, well
  chilled
Ice water

FOR THE FILLING:

1 cup sugar
1/4 cup water
1 1/2 teaspoons ground cinnamon
2 tablespoons butter
6 Granny Smith apples

2 tablespoons Calvados or light
  rum
6 cinnamon sticks
1 egg yolk beaten with 2
  teaspoons water for glaze
2/3 cup heavy cream, chilled

Make the piecrust by combining the flour, sugar, and salt in a bowl. Cut the butter into cubes and work it into the flour until the flour is the texture of fine meal. Add ice water by the tablespoon just until you are able to gather the dough into a neat, smooth ball. Flatten ball to a 1-inch-thick round. Cover with plastic wrap or foil and refrigerate for at least 30 minutes.

Make a cinnamon syrup by combining the sugar, water, cinnamon, and butter in a saucepan. Heat to a boil, then turn the heat down and simmer for 5 minutes. Remove from the heat. Preheat the oven to 350° F. Peel the apples, leaving them whole. Cut a neat round core down through the center. Place the apples in a buttered gratin or soufflé dish that holds them as snugly as possible. Stir the Calvados into the cinnamon syrup. Using a good half of the liquid, spoon the syrup down the center of each apple.

Roll out the pie dough on a floured surface until it is ¼ inch thick. Drape the dough loosely over the apples. Gently press the dough so that it drapes into the spaces between the apples. Tuck it in around the edge of the dish, then let it hang over the rim. Cut off a ½-inch overhang and crimp the dough around the edge of the dish in a nice pattern. Make a slit through the dough into the cored center of each apple and insert a cinnamon stick. Brush the dough with the egg yolk glaze. Bake the "pie" for around 45 minutes (if the top seems to be overbrowning, cover it with foil). To serve, whip the cream until it starts to thicken. Whip in the remainder of the cinnamon syrup. Dish out an apple per person with some of the crust, and pour the cinnamon cream over the top.

Season of mists and mellow fruitfulness!
Close bosom-friend of the maturing sun;
Conspiring with him how to load and bless
With fruit the vines that round the thatch-eaves run;
To bend with apples the mossed cottage-trees,
And fill all fruit with ripeness to the core;
To swell the gourd, and plump the hazel shells
With a sweet kernel; to set budding more,
And still more, later flowers for the bees,
Until they think warm days will never cease,
For Summer has o'erbrimmed their clammy cells.

—JOHN KEATS,
To Autumn

Her rash hand in evil hour
Forth reaching to the fruit, she plucked, she eat:
Earth felt the wound, and Nature from her seat,
Sighing through all her works, gave signs of woe
That all was lost.

—JOHN MILTON,
Paradise Lost

Key Lime Pie

*One 9-inch pastry shell, prebaked
and cooled*

FILLING

4 egg yolks, lightly beaten
*1 (14-ounce) can sweetened
condensed milk*

²/₃ cup fresh lime juice
Few drops green food coloring

TOPPING

*1 cup heavy cream, whipped
with 3 tablespoons superfine
sugar*

Beat yolks with condensed milk just to blend, add lime juice, and beat until smooth (the filling will be soft). Tint pale green and pour into baked pie shell. Chill well, then spread whipped cream topping over filling, making sure it touches pastry all around. Return to refrigerator and chill several hours before serving or, better still, overnight, so that filling will firm up somewhat (it will never really be firm).

Triple Melon

SERVES 2

1 cantaloupe, halved and deseeded
1 honeydew, halved and deseeded

2 tablespoons Midori or other
melon liqueur

With a melon baller, scoop balls from melons. With a small spoon, smooth out the cantaloupe halves and place equal amounts of honeydew and cantaloupe in the hollowed halves. Drizzle 1 tablespoon Midori over each "bowl."

Strawberries in Balsamic Vinegar

SERVES 3

1 pint strawberries, hulled and sliced

1 tablespoon balsamic vinegar

1 tablespoon superfine sugar

1 tablespoon orange juice

In a nonreactive bowl combine all ingredients. Divide on 3 shallow bowls and serve.

Fruit Chocolate Fondue

10 ounces white chocolate, broken
    into small pieces
$^1/_2$ cup heavy cream
2 tablespoons Grand Marnier

2 apples, cored and sliced
2 pears, cored and sliced
1 pint strawberries

In the top of a double boiler combine chocolate, heavy cream, and Grand Marnier. Place over simmering water and cook, covered, until smooth, stirring frequently. Remove from heat and serve immediately, dipping fruit into fondue.

And the fruits will outdo

what the flowers have promised.
—FRANÇOIS DE MALHERBE,
Prière pour le roi Henri le Grand

SOURCES

EXCERPTS

PHOTO CREDITS